MEDITATIONS

Growing in Friendship with God

WILLIAM A. BARRY, SJ

LOYOLA PRESS.
A JESUIT MINISTRY

Chicago

LOYOLA PRESS.
A JESUIT MINISTRY

3441 N. Ashland Avenue
Chicago, Illinois 60657
(800) 621-1008
www.loyolapress.com

Imprimi potest: Very Rev. Thomas J. Regan, SJ, provincial

With the exception of readings for Holy Thursday and Good Friday, all readings in this book are adapted from *A Friendship Like No Other* by William A. Barry (Chicago: Loyola Press, 2008).

Readings for Holy Thursday and Good Friday are adapted from *Changed Heart, Changed Mind* by William A. Barry (Chicago: Loyola Press, 2011).

Scripture quotations contained herein are from the New Revised Standard Version Bible: Catholic Edition, copyright © 1993 and 1989 by the Division of Christian Education of the National Council of the Churches of Christ in the U.S.A. Used by permission. All rights reserved.

Quotations from the Spiritual Exercises are taken from George E. Ganss, trans., *The Spiritual Exercises of Saint Ignatius: A Translation and Commentary* (St. Louis: Institute of Jesuit Sources, 1992). Used with permission of the Institute of Jesuit Sources.

Cover illustration Betelgejze/Shutterstock, cover texture, tusumaru, iStock, Thinkstock.

ISBN-13: 978-0-8294-4242-7
ISBN-10: 0-8294-4242-1
Library of Congress Control Number: 2014954342

Printed in the United States of America.

14 15 16 17 18 19 Courier 10 9 8 7 6 5 4 3 2 1

Contents

Fifth Week of Lent

Holy Week

Easter Triduum

How to Use This Book

Dear Reader:

   Thanks for picking up this little booklet. I hope it leads you into a closer relationship with God. The readings for each day of Lent are taken, for the most part, from *A Friendship Like No Other*, in which I converse with a reader about God's desire for our friendship. I am convinced that God wants a deep personal relationship with each one of us, and I hope that my book will lead many people to engage in such a personal and intimate relationship with God. For each day of Lent you will read a citation adapted from *A Friendship Like No Other* along with a question for prayer and/or reflection. I am delighted with the way Joseph Durepos of Loyola Press has arranged these citations for our Lenten journey.

   Lent is a great time to give God a chance to convince you of his desire for your friendship. Traditionally Lent has been a time of engaging in practices of penance or prayer that will ready us to experience, more and more deeply, the almost unbelievable love and generosity of God toward us wayward human beings. I hope you will make the reading and prayer of this booklet a part of your Lenten journey this year. The really nice thing about this practice is that it will not take a great deal of time from your busy day. But you will, I hope, find it enriching to spend a few minutes each day reading the citation and communicating with God about your reactions to the day's reflection. If you do this regularly, I can promise you that on Easter Sunday you will be on more friendly terms with God—Father, Son, and Holy Spirit.

William A. Barry, SJ

Friendship with God

I maintain that God—out of the abundance of divine relational life, not any need for us—desires humans into existence for the sake of friendship. This thesis may sound strange, because it runs counter to much teaching about God. To be honest, I questioned it myself when I first began to think it through. But over the years, as my own relationship with God has deepened and I have listened to people talk about how God relates to them, I have become convinced that the best analogy for the relationship God wants with us is friendship.

As I begin my Lenten journey, I pray to understand what it means for my life that God wants to be friends with me.

Embracing the Notion of Friendship with God

This notion of friendship with God seems to have waxed and waned throughout history. It is possible that preachers and teachers of religion fear that embracing the idea of friendship with God may lead to effacing the mystery and awesomeness of God, and so they hesitate to talk about it. But I am convinced that this is an idea whose time has come, and none too soon for the future of our world. Many people I have met seem drawn by the notion of friendship with God. For another, friendship with God leads to a wider and wider circle of friends as we realize that God's desire for friendship includes all people.

How does the idea that God desires to be in friendship with all people change my idea of God? How does it change the way I interact with the people in my life?

Overcoming Our Fear of God

The psalmist writes: "The fear of the LORD is the beginning of wisdom" (Psalm 111:10). But the fear of the LORD extolled in the psalm is a far cry from the fear instilled by religious teaching, which leads people to keep their distance from God. The psalms surely were not written to keep people far from God, but just as bad news sells better than good, so too, hellfire and brimstone make for more compelling teaching and preaching. But I believe that God is shortchanged by such teaching and preaching tactics, and so are we.

If I'm honest with myself, do I find that I fear God?
How does this fear affect my relationship with God?

The Beginning of Wisdom

The "fear of the LORD" that is the beginning of wisdom is a healthy realization of God's awesomeness. God is fascinating and awe-inspiring, even terrifying. But suppose for a moment that God, who is Mystery itself—awesome, terrible, and unknowable—wants our friendship. Then the beginning of wisdom might be an acceptance of God's offer, even though accepting it proves to be daunting, challenging, and even a bit frightening.

Am I ready to accept the Divine Mystery's offer of friendship?

First Week of Lent

The Meaning of Friendship

It might help your reflection on friendship with God to think about your friendships with others. Who are your friends? What makes you say that they are your friends? You tell them things about yourself that you would not tell a stranger. You know that they will not tell others the secrets you share with them, that they will not hold against you what you tell them or hold it over your head as a threat. At the deepest level, you trust that they will remain your friends even when they know some of the less savory aspects of your past life and your character. You also trust that they will stick with you through thick and thin, through good times and tough times. And at least some of these characteristics will also be true of the relationship God wants with you.

What is the most important characteristic I look for in a friend? Can I also find this characteristic in my friendship with God?

Discipleship

Once we get over the fear of God engendered by early training, we enter something like a honeymoon period with God. This is followed by a period of distance when we recognize how shamefully short we have fallen of God's hopes for us. The distance is closed when we realize that God loves us—warts and sins and all—and the friendship is solidified. We are able to be ourselves with God. Ultimately, we can become collaborators with God in God's family business. For Christians, this stage of collaboration in the family business is called discipleship.

Is there anything else I need to address before I can become a disciple of God?

God's Desire in Creating Us

When you experience uplifting of the heart—joy, and desire for "you know not what," as C. S. Lewis says—you are experiencing the deep desire within the human heart for friendship with God. This correlates with God's desire in creating us.

In my prayer today, I will seek to experience the deep desire within my heart for friendship with God.

The Lie at the Heart of Human Sinfulness

The lie at the heart of human sinfulness is that we can gain control of our existence by some action of our own and that God does not want us to have this power. God creating human beings in God's own likeness is described in the first creation account in Genesis. But instead of accepting the friendship with God that was offered, human beings chose to enter into rivalry with God. The consequences of that disastrous choice plague our world still.

Do I harbor any distrust of God over control and power in my life? Can I pray the New Testament prayer "I believe; help my unbelief"?

Attraction to God

St. Ignatius of Loyola believed that all human beings have experiences of God's creative and sustaining love. If we pay attention to these experiences, we will find that we desire God with all our heart and, at the same time, feel an enormous sense of well-being. Caught up in this experience, we feel that everything else and everyone else pales in comparison. We want this Mystery more than we want anything or anyone else.

God, today I pray to become more aware of your creative and sustaining love for me.

Disturbances in the Friendship

At some point in a friendship, one becomes aware that something is amiss, and the honeymoon is over. In the case of friendship with God, I know at this point that God has created me for friendship and wants a world in which human beings live harmoniously with God, with one another, and with the environment. But I realize that the world is not like this, and I have not lived up to God's dream, either—the world and I have fallen short of what God wants. A disturbance has been introduced into my friendship with God.

How have I not lived up to God's dream for me?

Through God's Eyes

As you become aware of where you have failed to live up to God's dream for you or where you have turned away from God's offer of friendship, speak to God. Notice how God reacts to your willingness to see yourself through God's eyes.

God, help me see myself through your eyes.

Second Week of Lent

Welcomed by God

When we can, in imagination, look Jesus in the eye—knowing that he sees us just as we are—and still find love and forgiveness, we feel a great sense of relief. People who ask God to show them their sins discover, to their delight, that along with the shame and tears they experience for the way they have lived, they are also freed of a tremendous burden. With a great sigh of relief they realize that God still loves them in their sinfulness and still wants their friendship. They have passed through the honeymoon period and the turmoil of realizing how far they have fallen short of what God wants, and they still feel loved and welcomed by God.

Jesus, give me the courage to look you in the eye and the grace to accept the love and forgiveness I find in your welcoming gaze.

The Heart of God

I have come to believe that the deepest movements of our hearts, those times when we are touched by the joys and sorrows of others, reflect the heart of God.

Compassionate God, help me open my heart to the joys and sorrows of others, and in so doing reflect your heart.

Coming to Know Jesus as a Friend

If you have entered a relationship of intimacy with God, you may now notice a change in your desire. You may want to engage more cooperatively in the divine purpose of creation. If you are a Christian, perhaps you want to know Jesus—in whose eyes you saw forgiveness and love—more intimately, to love him more ardently and follow him more closely. If this is your desire, you want Jesus to reveal himself, to let you know what makes him tick, what he loves and hates, what he dreams. Such revelation is the necessary condition for growing to love him and wanting to follow him.

Jesus, please reveal yourself to me more clearly so that I may love you more ardently and follow you more closely.

Contemplating the Gospels

In contemplating the Gospels during Lent, take this advice to heart: Be sure to take Jesus' humanity seriously even as you reflect on his divine attributes. God took humanity seriously enough to become one of us, and we do God a disservice if we downplay what God has done in becoming human. When we use our imagination in contemplating Jesus, we trust that God's Spirit will use it to reveal something about Jesus that is important for us so that we will love him and want to follow him. The only way we can get to know another person is through revelation; the other must reveal him- or herself to us. In contemplating the Gospels, we are asking Jesus to reveal himself to us.

Jesus, as I pray with Scripture this Lent, help me to be open to the revelation of your Spirit.

Thursday of the Second Week of Lent
Jesus as a Difficult Friend

As you get to know and love Jesus, you will notice that he meets you in unexpected ways. Jesus can be a difficult friend, one who challenges and makes demands as well as one who supports and comforts. The only way forward in this friendship is to tell Jesus what you really feel and think and then wait for his response. Jesus responds in different ways to different people. Most people who walk with Jesus in this contemplative way come to realize that following him is demanding and challenging.

How does the idea of Jesus as a demanding and challenging friend make me feel?

"I Wish I Had Known You Better."

How are you feeling about your relationship with Jesus? Do you know him better and like him more? Does he know you better and like to be with you? I was deeply moved during a retreat when one of the retreat leaders had us imagine someone meeting Jesus after death. The person says to Jesus, "I wish I had known you better in life." Jesus replies, "I wish I had known you better."

Jesus, help me to know you better, that you may know me better.

My Insignificance and God's Desire

One persistent source of resistance to God's desire for friendship is the notion that I am too insignificant to be of concern to God—except, of course, when I fail to live up to God's expectations. Then I am the object of God's anger. Even if I can be convinced that God does care for other people, I find it much harder to believe that God cares for me. As a result, I remain at a distance from God and consider myself justified, perhaps even virtuous, in maintaining that distance.

*Do I allow feelings of insignificance to distance
me from God?*

Third Week of Lent

Third Sunday of Lent
God Loves Us First

One of the biggest obstacles to an enduring relationship with God is our belief that the relationship depends, ultimately, on us. But God's love for us does not depend on us and what we do. God loves us first, and without any impetus on our part. God creates us for no other reason than God's love. So God's offer of friendship does not depend on our significance but solely on God's desire for us. I urge you to ask God to purge from your heart the vestiges of fear that produce feelings of insignificance and unworthiness. You do God no favor by thinking stingily or meanly about the person who is the apple of God's eye—you.

Loving God who created me, help me understand that I was created solely out of your desire and love for me.

Growing into Adulthood with God

I propose that the relationship between an adult child and his or her parent is a better image of the relationship God wants with us as adults. As we mature into adulthood, we become more like peers of our parents. We become more like equals as we take on the same adult roles they have had. I believe that this kind of relationship between an adult child and his or her parents is more like what God wants with us as we grow into adulthood.

How does the idea of relating to God as an adult child to a parent change the way I experience God?

God's Family Business

The story of creation shows that God's family business is not the church but the world. It is not reserved only for religious people, nor is it the work of individuals working independently. The family business into which we are invited as adult friends of God entails a community working together. We are all co-laborers in God's work of creation. The work cannot be accomplished without the cooperation of each one of us.

God, I ask for the grace to cooperate with others better and to see clearly that we are all part of the same creation.

God's Vulnerability

In Jesus, God saves us by becoming so vulnerable that we are able to kill him in a vile and humiliating way. The crucifixion and resurrection of Jesus assure us that God's offer of friendship will never be withdrawn, no matter what we do. If the cross did not result in a withdrawal of the offer, then nothing we do will lead to a change of God's heart. We can, however, refuse the offer. Friendship is a mutual relationship, and a person has to accept the offer; he or she cannot be coerced or tricked into it. And any human being's final refusal of God's friendship breaks God's heart. Still, God does not turn away from such a person in anger and rage. God lives eternally with a broken heart. That's how vulnerable God wants to be.

Loving God, I pray for the wisdom to never turn away from your friendship or take advantage of your love for me.

Thursday of the Third Week of Lent
Heart by Heart

If our salvation consists in accepting God's offer of friendship, then from the beginning of human existence on earth, God's plan for the world has entailed human acceptance of God's friendship. We turned away from this friendship and lost our way. We were in need of salvation from our folly. God's answer was to renew the offer of friendship and to send Jesus to share our lot and show us how to live as friends of God. Thus, the saving of the world comes about, heart by heart. God offers friendship to each human being not only as a path to his or her salvation but also as a means to the salvation of the world.

God's offer of friendship is my invitation not only to fullness of life but also to becoming part of the world's salvation.

A Large-Enough Heart

It is clear that the friendship God offers cannot be had in isolation from other human beings. Just as human friendship entails becoming friends of my friend's friends and family, becoming a friend of God involves accepting God's other friends, at least in principle. Mind you, God's other friends are potentially all the people on the planet. So my joy, my fulfillment, and my salvation consist in opening myself to friendship with God and with every man, woman, and child ever created. At the least, I must be open to conversation with God about having such a large heart.

God, give me the grace to see with a heart large enough to love as you do.

How God's Compassion Works

To be compassionate means to feel so profoundly for others who are in trouble or pain that we will put ourselves at risk to help them. That's how God's compassion works. We live in this world as God's images insofar as we show compassion for others in the way God shows compassion. Because God is the creator of all humanity and, indeed, of all creation, we must not limit our compassion to our own family, tribe, or nation.

Loving God, give me the grace and courage to extend compassion toward your creation as you do.

Fourth Week of Lent

Fourth Sunday of Lent

Compassion in Action

In a way, God had to show us how to become compassionate human beings by becoming one of us. In Jesus, God showed us compassion, and we have no excuse for not imitating Jesus in this. We can do it because God creates us for this role, gives us the Spirit to move our hearts and minds to such compassion, and gives us Jesus to show us the way: "I am the way, and the truth, and the life" (John 14:6). The future of our world depends on our willingness to live as the human beings God has created us to be—allowing our hearts to be touched by the plight of our fellow humans and taking action for the sake of the other.

Jesus who leads me, may the gift of compassion that you give freely to me guide me to live not simply for myself but for others in need.

Compassion for God

God creates and sustains all that exists, including sick and evil people who do incalculable harm to their fellow human beings. When I sense God's presence to the horrors I see in the world, I am often brought to tears. It's heartbreaking to think of God, the loving, compassionate One, witnessing the evil done in the world. Do you feel something like compassion *for God* as you consider this? What must it be like for God to be present to such events as we see in the news almost daily. If we can be moved to compassion, how much more must God be moved, who not only hears about what has happened but also is present, and who sustains even the perpetrators of such horrors.

God, I've never considered that being compassionate means extending compassion even to you—help me understand and be a witness in the world. May I be one who sees with your sustaining love and forgiveness.

Sharing the Burden

Yes, I have come to believe that friendship with God can lead us to have compassion for God. I have, of course, wondered whether I was being irreverent or presumptuous, and I have asked God to let me know if I was on the wrong track. So far, I have not experienced any response that would lead me to change my belief. Indeed, I sense that God is pleased that I share the burden. Moreover, I have found myself growing in the ability to listen with compassion to stories of horror. It is not easy to listen to such stories, but I find myself consoled and grateful that I am more able to do so. I wonder whether God is hoping for more and more adult friends who are willing to share God's own pain and thus grow in the ability to listen with compassion to others.

God, give me the grace to share more fully with you in difficult situations and with difficult people, even to share in your pain when you are present to harm and betrayal.

Job and the Question of Evil

I don't have an answer to the question of why there is so much evil and pain in this world. All I can do is encourage you to speak directly to God if you have questions about God's ways. Speak as one friend to another, even if anger is the only emotion you can voice. The book of Job, I believe, encourages such honest relating with friends and indicates that God is willing to respond, even if the response is not, at first hearing, as comforting as we might hope.

Loving God, help me read the book of Job with an open heart and mind, that I might come to peace, if not understanding, about the question of evil in the world.

God's Will

Even though we may know that God and God's ways are a mystery that only God can know, we still try to identify God's will in the workings of creation. Often when a catastrophe occurs, whether in the form of a natural disaster or a human evil, we hear people speak of God's will: "God willed this hurricane in order to strengthen us and to draw us closer to him." "God wanted your mother to die so that she would be happy in heaven, where she will watch over you." "God wills whatever happens to us for our good." Such explanations presume to know God's intention. I would prefer not to ascribe to God an intention I do not know, so suffering and evil remain mysteries that place me squarely before the question of who God is.

God, give me the grace to accept the mystery that lies at the heart of knowing you.

Does God Reveal the Divine Inner Life to Us?

I have suggested that mutual self-revelation is one of the central hallmarks of friendship. With my best friends, I want to be as honest as I can be about my inner life, especially as it bears on our friendship, and I hope that they will reciprocate. Is there a similar mutual self-revelation in our friendship with God? Does God reveal the divine inner life to us? Or does the analogy break down at this point? After all, one thing seems to be clear: if human beings think they comprehend God, they are wrong. When we see God face-to-face, it will be our delight, I believe, to realize that we can never fathom the divine Mystery.

God, give me the grace to be as honest in my relationship with you as I am in my relationships with my closest friends.

God Revealing God

That the world exists at all reveals something about God. God does not need the universe in order to be God. When we come to the awesome awareness that our world, and we in it, exist only because God wants our existence, we can begin to reflect on the One who does this. In creating the universe, God reveals God's self, since there is nothing else that could be a model. But we have to allow ourselves to be intrigued by the mystery that there is anything at all.

Creator God, help me fathom that the universe exists in part to reflect You who created it.

Fifth Week of Lent

Fifth Sunday of Lent

Sending His Spirit

People in the early church recalled that Jesus had spoken of sending his Spirit. Their transformation into a new way of being human could have come about only by the presence of God active in them as individuals and as a community. In this activity, God revealed that the relationality within God was threefold. This is how the people experienced God's friendship. They received the revelation of God as Trinity, not through some esoteric doctrine given to them as initiates in a special cult, but through God's saving action in creating and redeeming our world—hence, God reveals who God is in deeds more than in words.

God, help me experience your friendship in the same
way your followers in the early church did—help me
to be aware of how you reveal yourself in deeds
through your Spirit.

Where Do We Experience God?

If God wants our friendship, where do we experience God drawing us into such a relationship? I have suggested taking time to pray in an effort to recognize such experiences, but it may also help to spend some time reflecting on where you have experienced God already. It's my hope, indeed my prayer for you, that you will find God wherever you are. All you need to do is pay attention, and I consider paying attention an effective form of prayer.

God, grant me the grace in the midst of daily distractions to pause and pay attention, and in so doing, be aware that you love me.

Thin Places

For Christians, Jesus of Nazareth is the "place" where heaven and earth meet, where the holy is present uniquely and forever. The baptism of Jesus (Luke 3:21–22) and his transfiguration (Mark 9:2–13) exemplify how heaven and earth meet in him. In Jesus, God is so present that he is, in some mysterious way, both fully human and fully divine. To meet Jesus is to meet God. Jesus is "holy ground" par excellence. Where do we experience God? Where is our holy ground? The Irish speak of "thin places," where the border between heaven and earth, sacred and secular, seems especially porous and God is believed to "leak through" more easily. Because I believe that God can leak through anywhere, I prefer to say that in such places people find the presence of God more easily.

Where are the thin places in my life?

Scripture as a Thin Place

We should be aware of the thin places in our lives because they make experiences of God's desire for each one of us, and our desire for God, more possible by capturing our attention and pulling us out of our ordinary routines and concerns. Scripture, either heard or read, can be a thin place if we let the words capture our imagination and attention. Scripture will not be a thin place if we read it solely for meaning. All too often, we don't let the Scriptures do what they were written to do—namely, to give the Mystery we call God a chance to be heard and met.

Loving God, help me encounter you in the way the biblical writers intended: to engage you personally, to hear you, and to meet you in the Mystery of Scripture.

Liturgy as a Thin Place

When people gather together to celebrate their communion with God, the community this creates can be experienced as a thin place. There is something about the gathering of people for prayer—especially if they come from diverse families and backgrounds—that sets off sparks in those present, giving them a sense that they are on holy ground. For Christians, of course, the Eucharist is the gathering that most often is experienced as holy ground. This is all the more true when the Eucharist is celebrated with striking beauty and prayerfulness. If, in addition, the congregation is large and culturally and racially diverse, the experience can be even more moving, because we sense that God's dream—for a world in which all are one in friendship with God and with one another—is being fulfilled.

Jesus, give me the grace to experience liturgy as a thin place.

Friday of the Fifth Week of Lent

The Unlikeliest Thin Place

The unlikeliest thin place in all of history is Golgotha, where church and state conspired to kill an innocent man. Yet even here the Roman centurion who led the soldiers who crucified Jesus gasped, "Truly this man was God's Son!" (Mark 15:39). Ever since that awful and awesome day, Christians have contemplated Jesus on the cross and there have found God and hope and peace. It is unlikely indeed, yet a fact: we can find places where heaven and earth meet amid beauty or devastation, amid sorrow or joy. As the Jesuit poet Gerard Manley Hopkins put it: "The world is charged with the grandeur of God." Every place on this earth can be a thin place. All that is required to experience God is our openness to God's presence.

God of all, as I prepare for Holy Week, I ask you to grant me the grace to contemplate Golgotha as a thin place in all its sorrow and joy, a place where heaven and earth met amid beauty and devastation.

Spiritual Consolation

St. Ignatius believed that God wants us to be happy and fulfilled and that the way to be happy and fulfilled is to be in tune with God's dream for the world and for us. I believe that the way to be happy and fulfilled is to accept God's offer of friendship and to live in accordance with that friendship. If we are trying to do this, according to Ignatius, "consolation" is the order of the day. This does not mean that life will be without pain and suffering; it means that God wants to be a consoling presence to us even in the midst of life's inevitable pain and suffering.

Loving God, I ask for the grace of consolation in accepting your offer of friendship.

Holy Week

God's Spirit Moving in You

What, exactly, is consolation? Consolation refers to any experience of desire for God, of distaste for one's past sins, or of sympathy for Jesus or any other suffering person. It refers, in St. Ignatius's words, to "every increase in hope, faith, and charity, and every interior joy which calls and attracts one toward heavenly things and to the salvation of one's soul, by bringing it tranquility and peace in its Creator and Lord" (*The Spiritual Exercises*, n. 316). Paul's letter to the Galatians lists the fruit of the Spirit as "love, joy, peace, patience, kindness, generosity, faithfulness, gentleness, and self-control" (5:22–23). When you experience this group of movements in your being, you can be relatively sure that God's Spirit is moving in you.

God, I pray for the "love, joy, peace, patience, kindness, generosity, faithfulness, gentleness, and self-control" promised by St. Paul and given by your gracious Spirit.

Contemplating Jesus' Passion and Death

Contemplation of the Gospels during Lent with the desire to know Jesus better, love him more ardently, and follow him more closely, leads inevitably to the Crucifixion. When we walk with Jesus to Jerusalem, we find ourselves wanting to share in his passion and death, and perhaps dreading it.

Jesus, give me the courage to walk with you to Jerusalem and beyond.

Our Way of Proceeding

If we are trying to live as friends of God, we can trust that our experience is of God's Spirit when we find ourselves more alive, more peaceful, more energized, and also more concerned about others than about ourselves as a result of the experience. These simple rules of thumb are not absolute guarantees that we are right or that our way of proceeding will succeed, but they give us some assurance that we are on the right path. If we follow the impulses of such experiences, we can move forward with confidence, trusting that God will continue to show us the way.

Holy Spirit, as I move into Holy Week, let me follow your way of proceeding, and grant me the trust to know I'm moving with and toward you always.

Accepting the Offer

Throughout this Lenten journey, I have maintained that God wants all human beings to be "holy souls," and thus "friends of God, and prophets." I hope that you have experienced God's desire for your friendship and your corresponding desire to be God's friend. I am convinced that the only way to the fulfillment of God's dream for our world is for more and more human beings to accept God's offer of friendship and to begin to live out the consequences. God wants friendship with you and with me and with all our brothers and sisters in the world. That's what our Lenten journey is all about. So let's take the offer, shall we?

Loving God, I accept your offer of friendship.

Easter Triduum

God Is the Love That Forgives

The question of what it means to be a friend of God ultimately draws us toward the topic of forgiveness. If we live truly as friends of God, we are called to forgive those who have offended us. And given what we have experienced, we know that the future of our world depends on a critical mass of people learning to let go of hate and embrace forgiveness. To be human is to become part and parcel of human magnanimity and compassion as well as human betrayal, violence, and sin. Perhaps Paul was referring to this aspect of what it means for God to become human when he said, "For our sake he [God] made him [Jesus] to be sin who knew no sin, so that in him we might become the righteousness of God" (2 Corinthians 5:21). In other words, for Jesus, forgiveness was the way of life.

Jesus, I fervently pray to walk in the way
of forgiveness.

What Faith Makes Possible

Jesus lived a human life as God's true Son, overcoming the temptations all of us inherit by being born into this world. On Good Friday, Jesus went to his death trusting that his dear Father would bring victory out of what seemed the total defeat of his mission. In the garden on the night before his death, he seems to have faced for the last time the temptation to fear, but he was able to hand over his life in trust to his Father. He went to his death believing that his way of being Messiah was the way to bring about God's Kingdom, and he absorbed human evil without passing it on. His faith made this possible.

Jesus, help me face the evil of the world with the faith you demonstrated on Good Friday.

Contemplating the Resurrected Jesus

Facing the full impact of Jesus' humiliating and painful death on the cross is the only way to experience the real joy of the Resurrection. We ask to share the joy of Jesus resurrected from the dead, but the depth of that shared joy comes only after we share with Jesus something of what he experienced in his crucifixion. He still has the wounds, even in glory; the horror is not undone by the Resurrection. Rather, with the Resurrection we find that his crucifixion and death are not the last word. Here is a magnificent sign of God's forgiving love: even the worst we can do will not deter God from the desire to embrace us in friendship.

May the honest horror of the Crucifixion help bring me to a deeper celebration of the Resurrection.

Easter Sunday
Jesus Is Risen!

The joy of the Resurrection is that Jesus is alive and well, that God has raised him bodily from the dead, and that his resurrection will be ours. When you are given the grace to share in Jesus' joy through contemplation of the scenes of his resurrection, you can never despair, no matter what happens in your life, because you know in your bones that Jesus is risen and that you are one with him and will share in his resurrection.

Jesus, let the joy of the Resurrection be the enduring grace that guides my life.

Also available from
William A. Barry, SJ

A Friendship Like No Other: Experiencing God's Amazing Embrace

Paperback | 2702-8 | $14.95

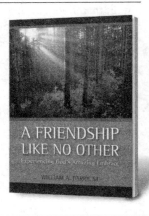

E xplore the path to becoming a friend of God. Grounded in biblical tradition and Ignatian spirituality, *A Friendship Like No Other* offers a fresh approach to becoming a friend of God and understanding this relationship.

Ignatian Spirituality Online

www.ignatianspirituality.com

Other Ignatian Titles:

What Is Ignatian Spirituality?
Paperback | 2718-9 | $12.95

A Simple, Life-Changing Prayer
Paperback | 3535-1 | $9.95

Radical Compassion
Paperback | 2000-5 | $17.95

TO ORDER: Call 800.621.1008, visit loyolapress.com/store
or visit your local bookseller.